John Harbison

NORTH AND SOUTH

(Six Poems of Elizabeth Bishop)

duration ca. 20'

AMP 8166

First Printing: December 2001

ISBN 978-0-634-01724-7

Associated Music Publishers, Inc.

DISTRIBUTED BY

HAL•LEONARD®
CORPORATION

7777 W. BLUEMOUND RD. P.O. BOX 13819 MILWAUKEE, WI 53213

North and South, Book I:

Ballad for Billie I
from Songs for a Colored Singer

A washing hangs upon the line,
      but it's not mine.
None of the things that I can see
      belong to me.
The neighbors got a radio with an aerial;
      we got a little portable.
They got a lot of closet space;
      we got a suitcase.

I say, "Le Roy, just how much are we owing?
Something I can't comprehend,
the more we got the more we spend…"
He only answers, "Let's get going."
Le Roy, you're earning too much money now.

I sit and look at our backyard
      and find it very hard.
What have we got for all his dollars and cents?
      –A pile of bottles by the fence.
He's faithful and he's kind
      but he sure has an inquiring mind.
He's seen a lot; he's bound to see the rest,
      and if I protest

Le Roy answers with a frown,
"Darling, when I earns I spends.
The world is wide; it still extends…
I'm going to get a job in the next town."
Le Roy you're earning too much money now.

Late Air

From a magician's midnight sleeve
      the radio-singers
distribute all their love-songs
over the dew-wet lawns.
      And like a fortune-teller's
their marrow-piercing guesses are whatever
you believe.

But on the Navy Yard aerial I find
      better witnesses
for love on summer nights.
Five remote red lights
      keep their nests there; Phoenixes
burning quietly, where the dew cannot climb.

Breakfast Song

My love, my saving grace,
your eyes are awfully blue.
I kiss your funny face,
your coffee-flavored mouth.
Last night I slept with you.
Today I love you so
how can I bear to go
(as soon I must, I know)
to bed with ugly death
in that cold, filthy place,
to sleep there without you,
without the easy breath
and nightlong, limblong warmth
I've grown accustomed to?
–Nobody wants to die;
tell me it is a lie!
But no, I know it's true.
It's just the common case;
there's nothing one can do.
My love, my saving grace,
your eyes are awfully blue
early and instant blue.

North and South, Book II:

Ballad for Billie II
from Songs for a Colored Singer

The time has come to call a halt;
        and so it ends.
        He's gone off with his other friends.
        He needn't try to make amends,
this occasion's all his fault.
        Through rain and dark I see his face
        across the street at Flossie's place.
        He's drinking in the warm pink glow
        to th'accompaniment of the piccolo.*

The time has come to call a halt.
I met him walking with Varella
and hit him twice with my umbrella.
Perhaps that occasion was my fault,
but the time has come to call a halt.

Go drink your wine and go get tight.
        Let the piccolo play.
        I'm sick of all your fussing anyway.
        Now I'm pursuing my own way.
I'm leaving on the bus tonight.
        Far down the highway wet and black
        I'll ride and ride and not come back.
        I'm going to go and take the bus
        and find someone monogamous.

The time has come to call a halt.
I've borrowed fifteen dollars fare
and it will take me anywhere.
For this occasion's all his fault.
The time has come to call a halt.

*Jukebox

Song

Summer is over upon the sea.
The pleasure yacht, the social being,
that danced on the endless polished floor,
stepped and side-stepped like Fred Astaire,
is gone, is gone, docked somewhere ashore.

The friends have left, the sea is bare
that was strewn with floating, fresh green weeds.
Only the rusty-sided freighters
go past the moon's marketless craters
and the stars are the only ships of pleasure.

"Dear, My Compass…"

Dear, my compass
still points north
to wooden houses
and blue eyes,

fairy-tales where
flaxen-headed
younger sons
bring home the goose,

love in hay-lofts,
Protestants, and
heavy drinkers…
Springs are backward,

but crab-apples
ripen to rubies,
cranberries
to drops of blood,

and swans can paddle
icy water,
so hot the blood
in those webbed feet.

–Cold as it is, we'd
go to bed, dear,
early, but never
to keep warm.

Program Note:

  North and South is a cycle of six settings of poems by Elizabeth Bishop composed between 1995 and 1999. It is divided into two books, each of similar proportion. Book One, dedicated to Lorraine Hunt Lieberson, begins with the first of Bishop's *Four Songs for a Colored Singer*. In an interview with Ashley Brown, Bishop said, "I was hoping someone would compose the tunes for them. I think I had Billie Holiday in mind. I put in a couple of big words just because she sang big words well… As for music in general; I'd love to be a composer." After this rhetorical opening comes a setting of a typically elusive love-and-loneliness Bishop incantation, *Late Air*. The third song, *Breakfast Song*, was not published. It was transcribed, in progress, by Lloyd Schwartz during a visit to Bishop while she was in the hospital.

  Book Two, dedicated to Janice Felty, begins with another, even more emphatic, declamation from *Songs for a Colored Singer*. It is followed by *Song*, a poem from the time of *North & South*, Bishop's first book, but published later. Finally, another very private lyric, *Dear, My Compass…*, which was discovered by Lloyd Schwartz in an inn in Ouro Preto, Brazil, an 18th-century mountain town where Bishop bought a house in 1965. Schwartz writes, "Here is the unmistakable voice of Elizabeth Bishop, here the fairy-tale vividness and coloring-book clarity of images… ; the geographical references – and restlessness – of the world traveler, the delicate yet sharply etched jokes… the apparent conversational casualness disguising the formality of the versification; the understated yet urgent sexuality; even the identification with animals."

John Harbison

North and South, as composed for voice and piano, was premiered at the Token Creek Festival
September 3, 2000 with Janice Felty, mezzo-soprano and Craig Smith, piano.

A chamber version *of North and South,* commissioned by The Chicago Chamber Musicians,
was premiered May 13, 2001 with Lorraine Hunt Lieberson, mezzo-soprano,
and is scored for voice with the following instruments:

English Horn
Clarinet in B♭
Bassoon
Violin
Viola
Violoncello
Contrabass

G. Schirmer Rental Department
P.O. Box 572
445 Bellvale Road
Chester, NY 10918
(845) 469-2271
(845) 469-7544 (fax)

NORTH AND SOUTH

for Lorraine Hunt Lieberson

BOOK I

Elizabeth Bishop

John Harbison

Ballad for Billie I

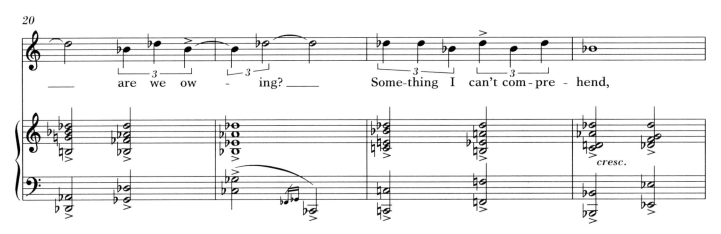

fence. He's faith - ful and he's kind ___ but he sure has _____ an in-quir - ing

mind. He's seen a lot; _____ he's bound_ to see the

In tempo

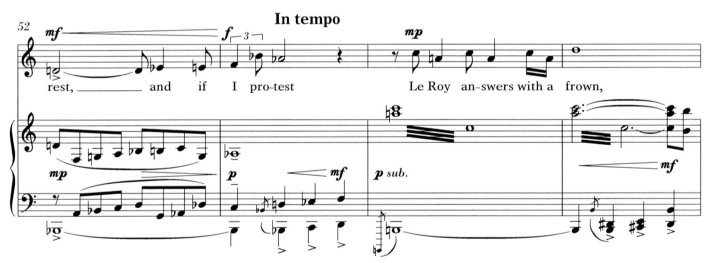

rest, _____ and if I pro-test Le Roy an-swers with a frown,

"Dar-ling,_ when I earns _____ I spends. The world is

wide; _____ it still _____ ex - tends... ___ I'm going to

get a job ___ in the next town." _____

Più sostenuto   **Free**

Le Roy,   you're earn-ing   too much mon-ey   now. _____

rit.

Late Air

Poco allegro ♩ = 92

From a ma-gi-cian's mid-night sleeve   the ra-di-o sing-ers

dis-trib-ute all   their love-songs   o - ver the dew - wet

lawns.   And like a

for - tune tel - ler's _____ their mar _____ -

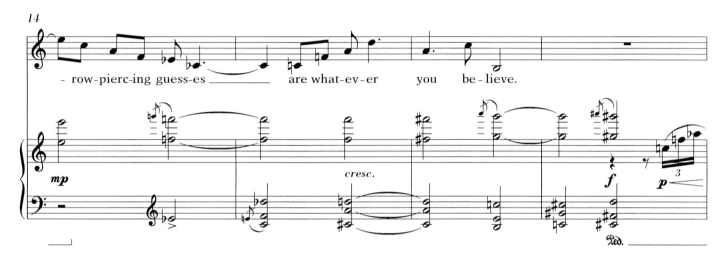

- row-pierc-ing guess-es _____ are what-ev-er you be-lieve.

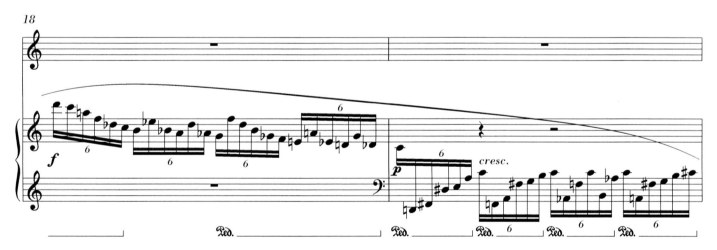

But on the Na - vy Yard ae-ri-al _____ I find bet-ter

wit-ness-es__ for love _____ on sum-mer

nights. ____ Five re - mote red lights ___ keep their nest there;

Phoe - nix - es burn - ing qui - et - ly, ___ where the dew can-not

climb. _____

Breakfast Song

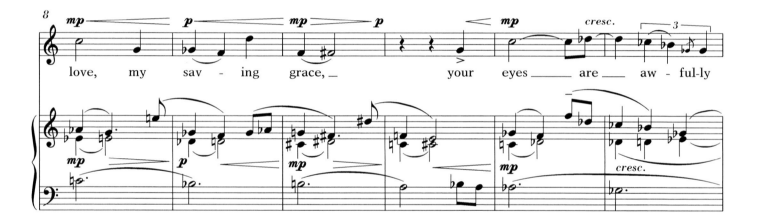

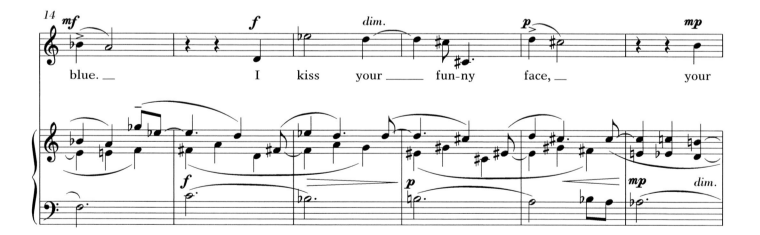

cof-fee - fla-vored _ mouth. Last night _ I slept with you. ____

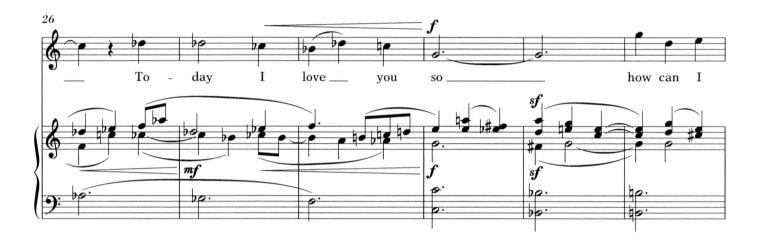

____ To - day I love __ you so ____ how can I

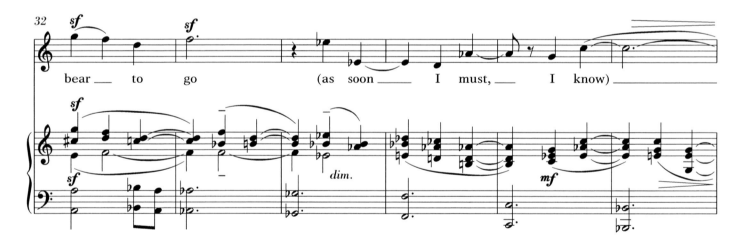

bear __ to go (as soon ___ I must, ___ I know) ____

_____ to bed ____ with ug - ly death _____ in that

cold, _____ filth - y place, _____ to

sleep there ___ with - out you, ___ with - out ___ the eas - y

breath _____ and night - long ___ limb-long warmth I've grown ac - cus - tomed

Misterioso

to? _____ No-bod - y

col 𝄢.

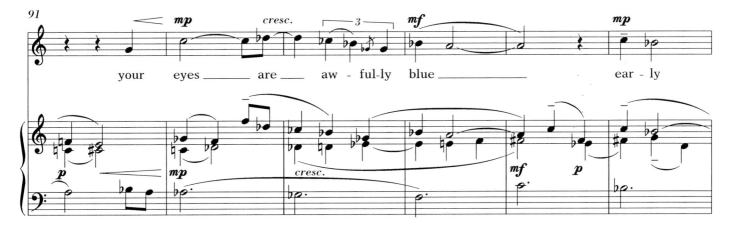

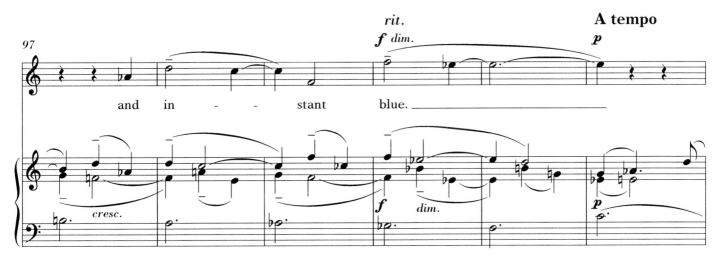

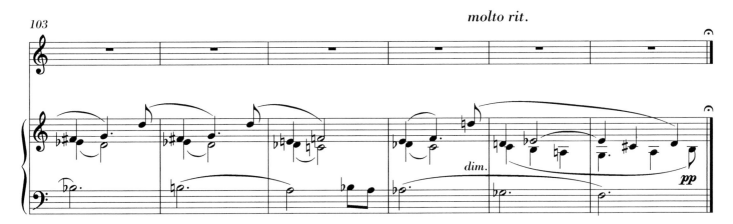

for Janice Felty

BOOK II

Ballad for Billie II

Lilting ♩ = 104

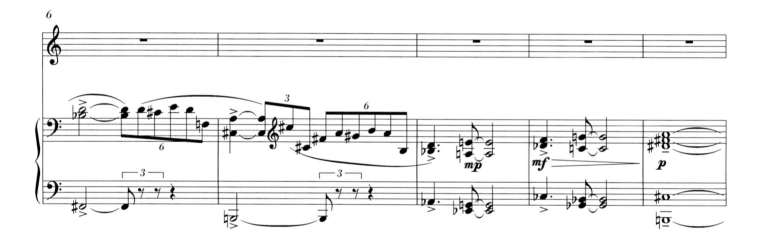

The time has come to call a halt; _____ and so it ends. _

He's gone off ____ with his oth-er friends. He need-n't try ____ to make a -

mends, ____ this oc - ca-sion's all his fault. ____ Through rain

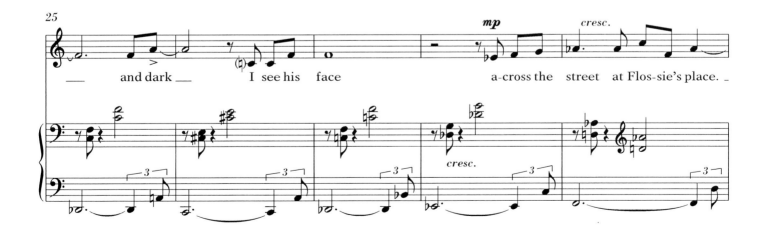

____ and dark ____ I see his face a-cross the street at Flos-sie's place. ____

He's drink-ing in the warm pink glow ___ to the ac-

com-p'ni-ment of the pic - co-lo.*

The time has come to call a halt._

I met him walk-ing with Va - rel-la and hit him twice with my um -

* Jukebox.

brel-la. Per-haps ____ that oc - ca-sion was my fault,

but the time has come ____ to call a halt. _

Go drink your wine and go get tight. Let the pic-co-lo play.

I'm sick ____ of all your fuss-ing an-y-way. _ Now I'm pur -

su-ing my own way. _____ I'm leav-ing _____ on the bus to-night. _____

_____ Far _____ down the high-way wet and black__ I'll ride __ and ride __

_____ and not come back. _____ I'm going to go _____ and

take the bus _____ and find some-one mo - nog-a-mous. __

The time has come to call a halt. ___ I've bor-rowed

fif-teen dol-lars fare _____ and it will take me an-y - where. ___ For this oc -

ca-sion's all his fault. ___ The time has come to call a halt. _

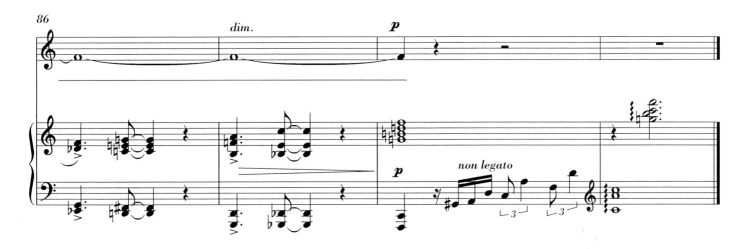

Song

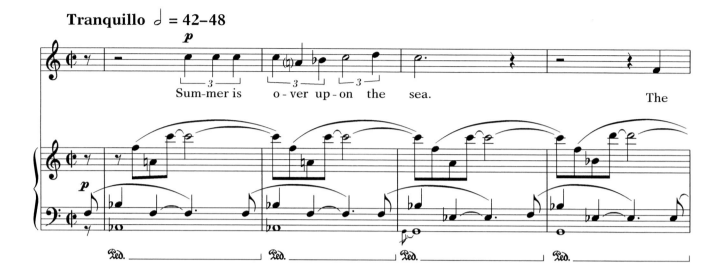

Tranquillo ♩ = 42–48

p

Sum-mer is o - ver up - on the sea.   The

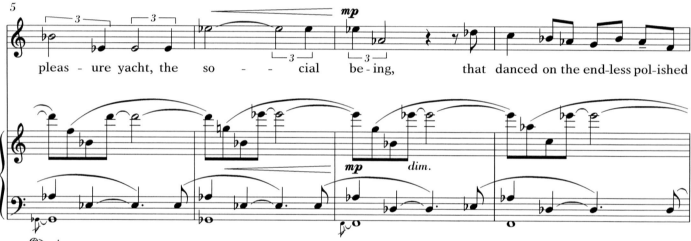

pleas - ure yacht, the so - - cial be - ing,   that danced on the end-less pol-ished

floor,   stepped   and side-stepped like Fred As-taire,   is gone, __

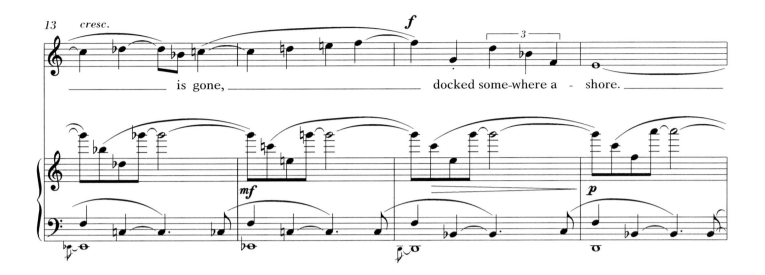

is gone, docked some-where a - shore.

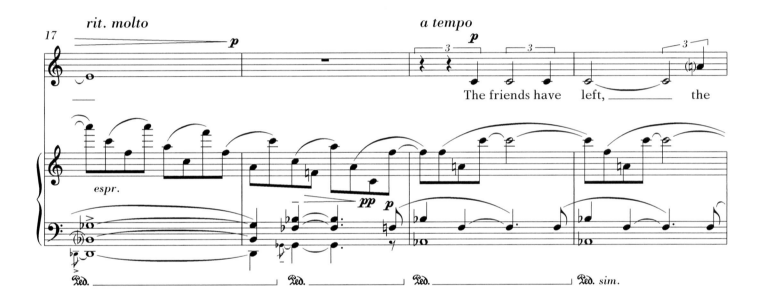

The friends have left, the

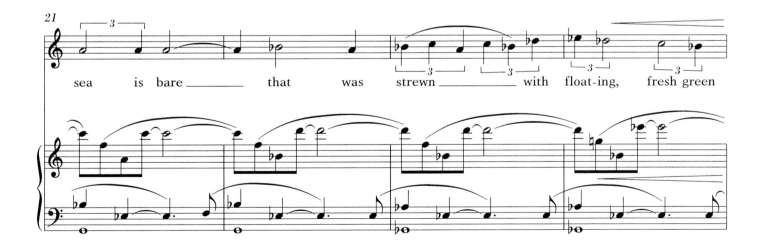

sea is bare that was strewn with float-ing, fresh green

weeds. On-ly the rust-y-sid-ed freight-ers go past _____ the

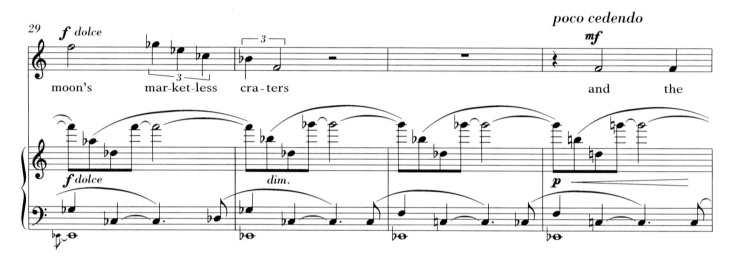

moon's mar-ket-less cra-ters and the

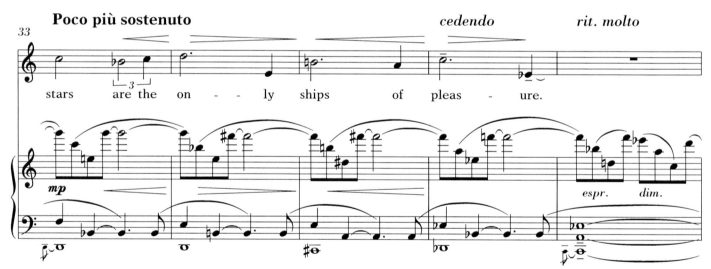

stars are the on - - ly ships of pleas - ure.

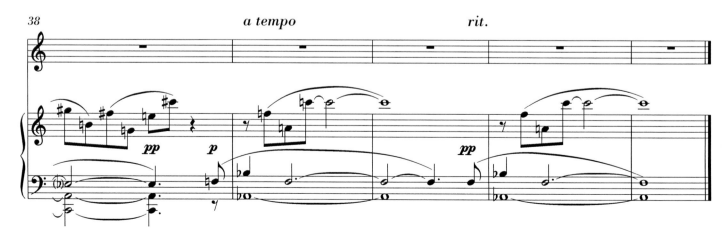

"Dear, My Compass…"

Grazioso, leggiero ♩ = 66

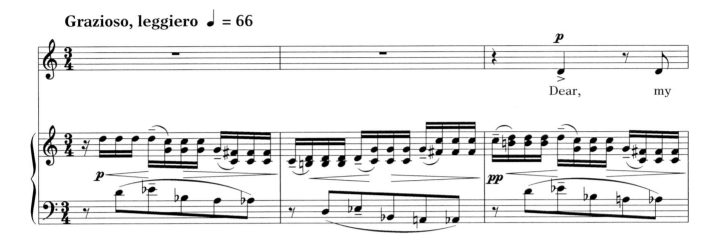

Dear, my

com-pass still points north to

cedendo **Tempo I**

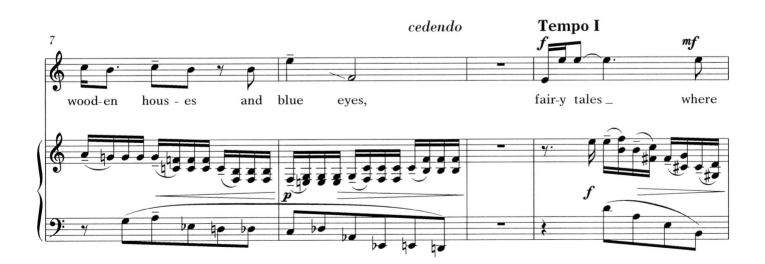

wood-en hous-es and blue eyes, fair-y tales _ where

24

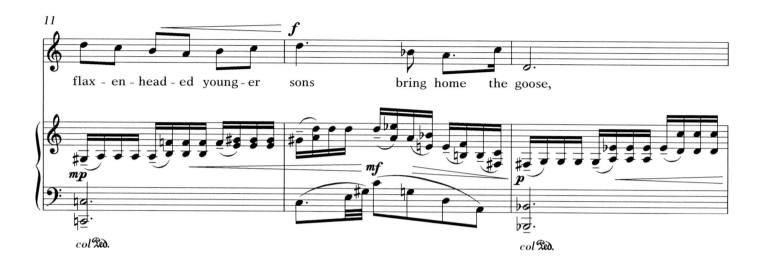

Springs are back-ward, but crab - ap - ples rip -

- en to ru - bies, cran - ber-ries to drops of blood, ____

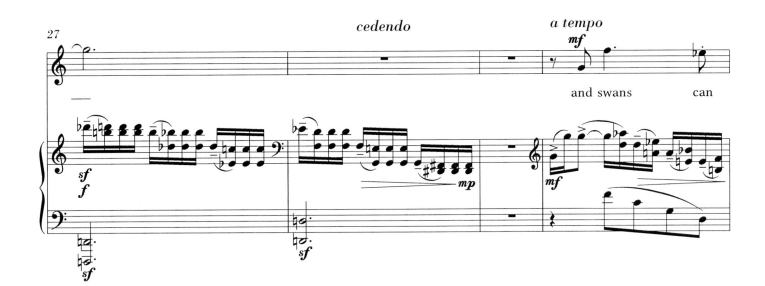

____ and swans can

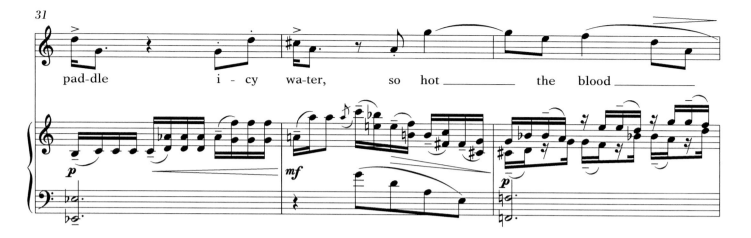

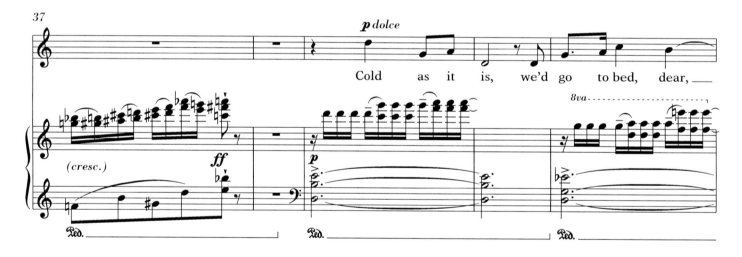